Wishing Traditions around the World

by M. J. Cosson • illustrated by Elisa Chavarri

Published by The Child's World®
1980 Lookout Drive • Mankato, MN 56003-1705
800-599-READ • www.childsworld.com

Acknowledgments
The Child's World®: Mary Berendes, Publishing Director
Red Line Editorial: Editorial direction
The Design Lab: Design
Amnet: Production

Design elements: Shutterstock Images

Photographs ©: Kevin Klöpper/iStockphoto, Cover, Title; Javier Rosano/
Shutterstock Images, 5; Ackab Photography/Shutterstock Images, 9;
Shutterstock Images, 11; Lidia Rakcheeva/iStockphoto, 15; PRILL
Mediendesign und Fotografie/Shutterstock Images, 20; Rena Schlid/
Shutterstock Images, 21; Hilary Brodey/iStockphoto, 25; Aldo Murillo/
iStockphoto, 27; Albert Barr/Shutterstock Images, 29

ISBN 9781614734314
LCCN 2012946515

Printed in the United States of America
Mankato, MN
November, 2012
PA02145

About the Author

M. J. Cosson has written many books
for children. She lives in the Texas hill
country with her husband, dogs, and
cat. She has five grandchildren, Jayna,
Averie, Gavin, Tristan, and Bethany, and
she wishes that their (and your) best and
bravest wishes come true.

About the Illustrator

Elisa Chavarri is a Peruvian illustrator
who works from her home in Alpena,
Michigan, which she shares with her
husband, Matt, and her cat, Sergeant
Tibbs. She has previously illustrated *Fly
Blanky Fly*, by Anne Margaret Lewis, and
Fairly Fairy Tales, by Esmé Raji Codell.

Table of Contents

Chapter One

Make a Wish

People make a wish on a star or when blowing out birthday candles. People say "I wish I had" or "I wish I could." People often sign cards and letters *best wishes*. What are they doing? What is a wish?

Making a wish is saying you want something. It is probably something that is not in your power to get. You might wish for a new toy or new shoes. You might not have the money to buy them yourself, but you hope somehow to get them. You might wish for a sunny day. You can't make that happen. But maybe if you wish for it, it will come true.

Wishing is something most people do. Wishing is like dreaming. What would life be like if you lived in a different place? What if you had a giraffe for a pet? What if you could visit Saturn?

Does wishing really make a wish come true? People all over the world have been making wishes for a long time. Does it help? What do you think?

Have you ever made a wish on a star?

Chapter Two

Stories about Wishing

Countries all over the world have stories about wishing. One story about wishing is "Aladdin's Wonderful Lamp." A boy, Aladdin, finds a very old lamp. When he rubs it a **genie** appears. Aladdin makes a wish and the genie grants it. Aladdin becomes rich. He marries the emperor's daughter. This story came from the Middle East. It might be more than a thousand years old.

Another story about wishing is "Cinderella." Cinderella is a kind, poor girl who wears rags. She does all the hard work around the house. One day the king has a ball. Cinderella wishes she could go. Her fairy godmother appears. She grants Cinderella's wish. Cinderella meets the handsome prince. She lives happily ever after.

This old story is told in different ways all over the world. It has different names, but the idea is the same. A kind but poor girl gets her wish.

Chapter Three

Coins in the Water

People have thrown coins in wells for hundreds of years. Ancient people believed there was a god or goddess in the water. People threw in coins to ask for favors from the god or goddess.

People throw coins in fountains to make wishes, too. Most fountains in a public place have coins in them.

The Trevi Fountain is in Rome, Italy. It is a very old and beautiful fountain. The statue of the god Ocean stands in the middle of the fountain. Other statues are called **Abundance** and Health. A visitor who wishes to return to Rome throws a coin in the Trevi Fountain. It is said that the fountain will grant his or her wish.

The Upwey Wishing Well in England is also very old. It has been a favorite place of kings and queens of England. People make a wish and toss in a coin.

People throw coins in the Trevi Fountain in Rome, Italy.

Chapter Four

Paper Cranes

The crane is a special bird in Japan. It is said to live for 1,000 years. In Japan, people believe your wish will come true if you fold 1,000 paper cranes. The art of **origami** is used to fold the paper cranes. There are many steps in folding them. It takes a long time to fold 1,000 paper cranes.

Today, children all over the world fold paper cranes to help others. Each crane holds a child's wish. Some cranes are folded to wish sick children well. Some are folded in the name of peace on earth.

A **tsunami** happened in Japan in 2011. It caused a lot of damage. Children folded paper cranes to help the people of Japan.

*People made wishes with paper cranes
for Japan after the tsunami.*

Chapter Five

Wishing Walls

Wishing walls are very, very old. They are important to many people. People write prayers and wishes on pieces of paper. They fold the papers and stick them in cracks in the walls. There is a famous wishing wall in Kusadasi in Turkey.

Times Square is in New York City in the United States. Every New Year's Eve there is a huge party there. At midnight, **confetti** rains down. Before New Year's Eve many people make wishes. They write their wishes on colorful paper. They pin them to a wishing wall in New York. The paper is gathered. It is used as confetti on New Year's Eve.

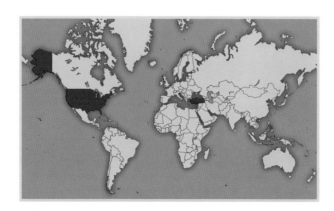

Chapter Six

Wishing Trees

The island of Cyprus has many wishing trees. Some are big, old trees. Some are bushes. They all have pieces of cloth tied to them. A person with a wish can tie a piece of cloth to the tree. He or she makes a wish while tying the knot.

In Wales, tree trunks are also wishing trees. Big, old trees that have been cut down or have fallen over are full of coins. People use a rock to pound a coin into the tree trunk as they make a wish.

People tie ribbons to this wishing tree in Finland.

Chapter Seven

The Moon

People say that if you make a wish on the full moon, your wish will come true. People wish on the moon all around the world. Some people wish on the blue moon. A blue moon happens when there is the second full moon in one month. The blue moon is special because it does not happen often.

People in South Korea **celebrate** the **harvest** moon. It is the eighth full moon of their calendar. This holiday is called *Chuseok* (CHOO-suhk). Many other Asian countries have moon festivals, too. They celebrate the harvest. People take walks and look at the moon. They might make a wish on the full moon.

Many moon wishes have to do with money. Some people hold a silver coin when they wish on the moon. Sometimes the full moon looks like a silver coin. Other people hold up purses or wallets to the **crescent** moon. They ask the moon to fill their purses with money.

Chapter Eight

Eyelashes

In Jamaica, if a person sees an eyelash that has fallen out, she can pick it up on her thumb. Then the person who found the eyelash and the person who lost the eyelash put their thumbs together. They each make a wish. Then they pull their thumbs apart. The person whose thumb the eyelash sticks to is the lucky one. That person's wish will come true.

There are other ways to make a wish on an eyelash. The person who lost the eyelash gets to make the wish. He puts it on the back of his hand. He closes his eyes and makes a wish. While his eyes are closed he gently blows the eyelash. If the eyelash is gone when he opens his eyes, the wish will come true.

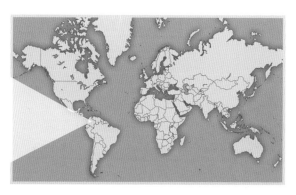

Chapter Nine

Dandelion Fluff

Dandelions are yellow flowers. Most people call them weeds. When the dandelion is old, the yellow turns to fluff. Each piece of fluff is a dandelion seed.

A person picks a dandelion when it is full of fluff. He or she makes a wish and blows the dandelion fluff. If all the fluff blows away, the wish will come true. This was a **tradition** in England. Then it came to the United States.

Rainbows

Rainbows are beautiful and rare. People in many places wish on rainbows. People in the Philippines wish for happiness when they see a rainbow.

In Ireland, people wish for money when they see a rainbow. They say there is a pot of gold at the end of the rainbow.

Ladybugs for Luck

Ladybugs bring good luck in many parts of the world. People make a wish on ladybugs. Many say this poem when they see a ladybug:

"Ladybug, ladybug, fly away home.

Your house is on fire and your children will burn."
When the ladybug flies off, the wish will come from the direction the ladybug flies.

In northern China, people make a 100-wishes **quilt** for a baby's birth. The quilt is called a *bai jia bei* (BYE JYAH BAY). One hundred friends and family members each make a wish on a piece of fabric. Someone sews them together to make a quilt. Fabric with ladybugs printed on it is popular for the 100-wishes quilt.

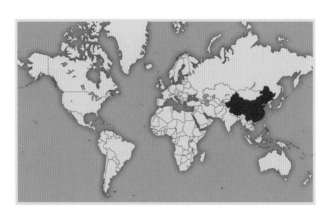

Chapter Twelve

Wishbones

A wishbone is from the breastbone of a bird. When the meat is gone, people clean the wishbone. Then they let it dry. In Italy thousands of years ago, people touched the dry bone and made a wish.

People in the United States celebrate Thanksgiving Day. Thanksgiving Day is in November. Eating turkey is a tradition. Later people wish on the wishbone. Two people hold the dry bone. They should hold it in the same place on opposite sides. Each person makes a wish. They pull the bone apart. The one who gets the larger piece of the bone gets his or her wish.

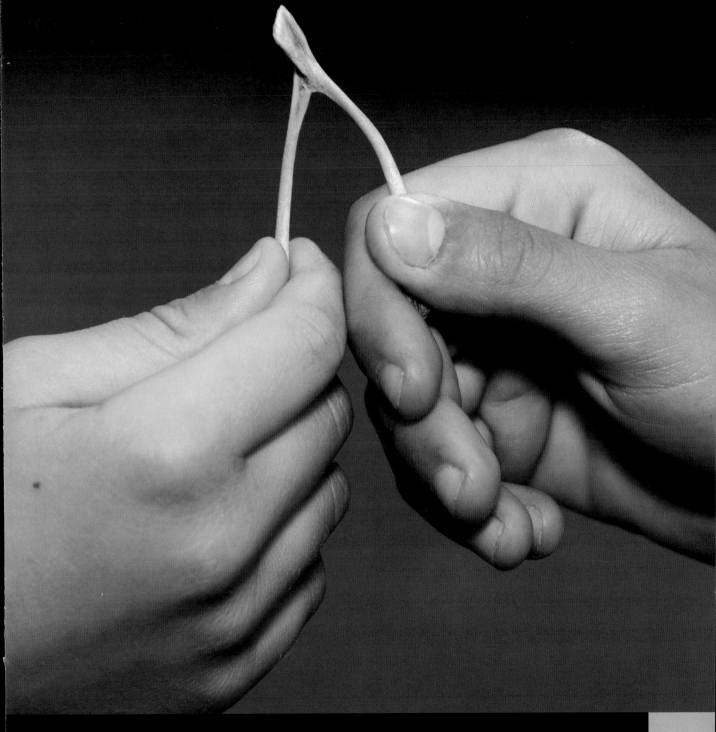

It is a tradition to break the wishbone on Thanksgiving.

Chapter Thirteen

Birthday Candles

Modern birthday parties began hundreds of years ago in Germany. Germans made birthday cakes for children. One big candle was placed in the center. The child made a wish and blew out the candle. The same candle was used for 12 years.

Today people around the world blow out birthday candles. They use one candle for every year. If a child turns eight, there are eight candles on the cake. The candles are lit. Everyone sings "Happy Birthday." The birthday person makes a wish and blows. If the candles are blown out in one breath, the wish will come true.

Make a wish and blow out the candles!

Up Close

People all over the world see the stars. Most people like to wish on them. You can wish on a falling star. Or you can wish on the first star. When you see the very first star in the evening sky, say this poem.

Star light, star bright,
First star I've seen tonight.
I wish I may
I wish I might
Have the wish I wish tonight.

Then close your eyes. Make your wish. Not telling is said to help your wish come true. American children have said this poem for more than 100 years.

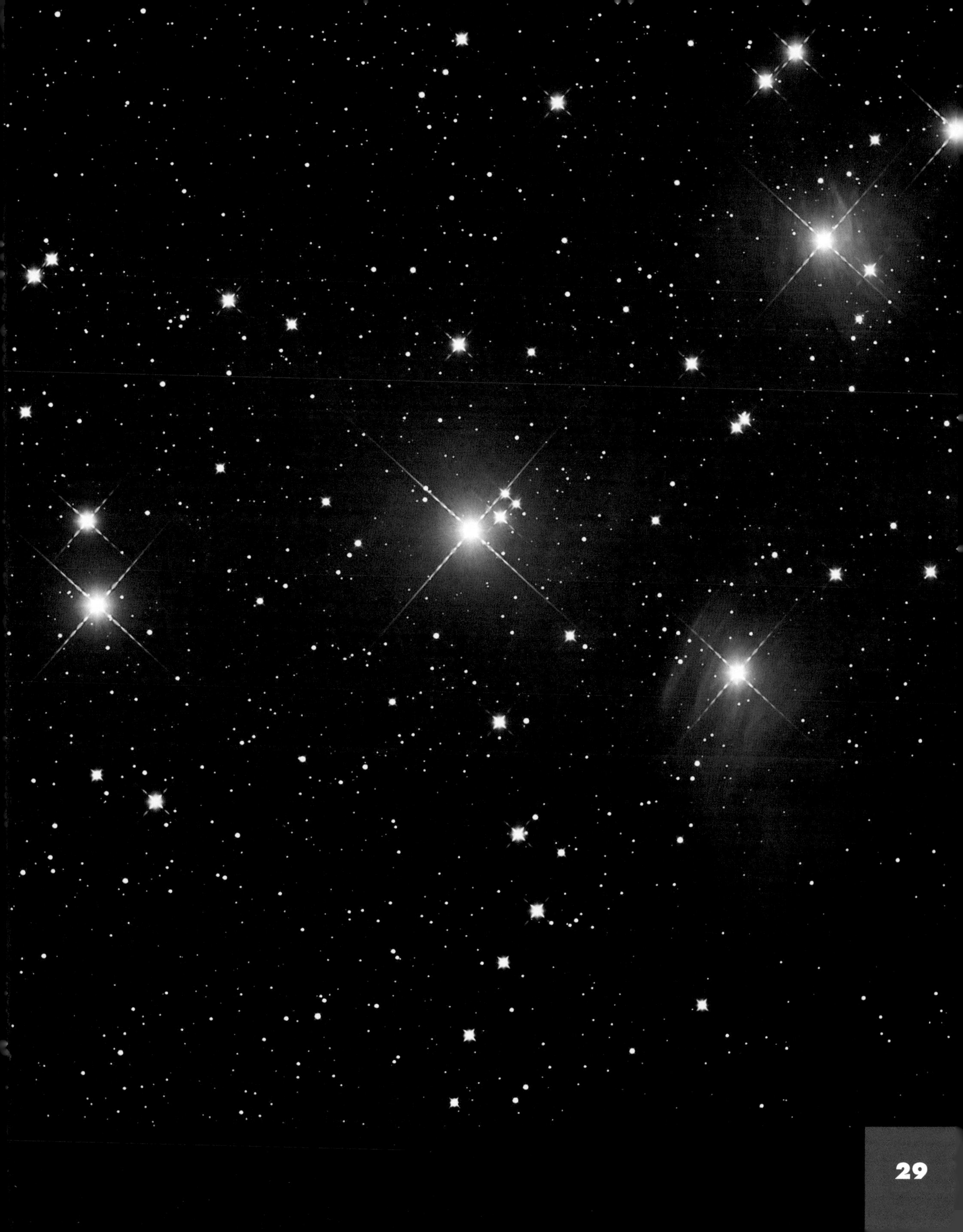

You can make a quilt like people in northern China make for a new baby. This project can be done alone or with a group.

Supplies:
large paper or poster board
magazines, gift wrap, colored paper, wallpaper samples
markers, crayons, colored pencils
scissors
ruler
glue stick or paste

Directions
1. Draw a design on the large paper or poster board. The design should have 100 pieces. It can be squares, triangles, or any shapes you want. It can even be a picture with exactly 100 parts.
2. Choose paper, gift wrap, or wallpaper for the shapes you drew. Some shapes might have a design or picture such as a ladybug, star, or the moon.
3. Cut the paper to fit into the shapes on the large paper.
4. Write a wish on each piece of paper.
5. Paste the wishes onto the large paper.
6. When your quilt is finished, place it where you can see it and think about the wishes.

Glossary

abundance (uh-BUHN-dunce) Abundance is having as much of something as you need or want. The statue stood for abundance.

celebrate (SEL-uh-brate) To celebrate is to observe or take notice of a special day. People celebrate birthdays with cake.

confetti (kuhn-FET-ee) Confetti is a large amount of small pieces of colored paper that are thrown or dropped on a crowd. People throw confetti on New Year's Eve.

crescent (CRES-unt) A crescent is a curved shape. The moon is shaped like a crescent when it is thin.

genie (JEE-nee) A genie is a magical spirit that grants wishes in some stories. The genie granted Aladdin's wish.

harvest (HAR-vist) Harvest is the time of year when crops are picked. Koreans celebrate the moon during the harvest.

origami (or-i-GAH-mee) Origami is the art of folding paper. Make a wish with an origami crane.

tradition (truh-DISH-uns) A tradition is a way of thinking or acting communicated through culture. People around the world have wishing traditions.

tsunami (tsu-NAH-mee) A tsunami is a huge wave caused by an underwater earthquake. There was a tsunami in Japan in 2011.

Learn More

Books

Thong, Roseanne. *Wish: Wishing Traditions Around the World*. San Francisco: Chronicle Books, 2008.

Web Sites

Visit our Web site for links about wishing traditions around the world: ***childsworld.com/links***

Note to Parents, Teachers, and Librarians: We routinely verify our Web links to make sure they are safe and active sites. So encourage your readers to check them out!

Index